The Home Stretch:

Matthew's Vision Of Servanthood In The End-Time

Gospel Sermons
For Sundays After Pentecost
(Last Third)

Cycle A

Mary Sue Dehmlow Dreier

CSS Publishing Company, Inc., Lima, Ohio

THE HOME STRETCH:
MATTHEW'S VISION OF SERVANTHOOD IN THE END-TIME

Scripture quotations are from the *New Revised Standard Version of the Bible,* copyright 1989 by the Division of Christian Education of the National Council of the Churches of Christ in the USA. Used by permission.

Library of Congress Cataloging-in-Publication Data

Dehmlow Dreier, Mary Sue, 1951-
 The home stretch : Matthew's vision of servanthood in the end time : Gospel sermons for Sundays after Pentecost (last third), cycle A / Mary Sue Dehmlow Dreier.
  p. cm.
 Includes bibliographical references.
 ISBN 0-7880-1826-4 (alk. paper)
 1. Pentecost season—Sermons. 2. Bible. N.T. Matthew—Sermons. 3. Bible. N.T. Gospels—Sermons. 4. Sermons, American—21st century. I. Title.
BV4300.5 .D44 2001
252'.64—dc21   2001025106
                                                                                CIP

For more information about CSS Publishing Company resources, visit our website at www.csspub.com.

ISBN 0-7880-1826-4   PRINTED IN U.S.A.

To my husband Gary,
my soul mate and preaching inspiration.

And to our children Betsy, Sarah, and Jake,
that you may each continue in such
challenging, insightful, and lively faith.

Acknowledgments

Preaching is hard work for me.

It is like giving birth: the struggle is certain and the outcome is completely in God's hands. There's relief when it's over, which I will certainly feel when I mail these sermons off to CSS! But mostly there's joy, not because the task is completed but because the gospel faithfully gives birth to new life.

To you, the reader of these sermons: Our times are calling for the message of these closing chapters of Matthew! These parables and sayings of Jesus both mobilize us to serve and call us to keep our vision on the promised fulfillment. Too often in our time faith becomes focused on one or the other. Matthew's community was called to both. So are we.

Writing these sermons has been a community effort.

To *People of Hope*, a Lutheran Church in Mission, ELCA, that Gary and I serve as mission pastor/developers: *Thank you* for all your responses to these sermons written on those infamous 3x5 cards. No, they weren't just a trick to make you pay attention! Your faith, insights, and honest critiques have greatly improved these sermons as well as helped me grow as a preacher among you. These are *your* sermons.

To Kay Alme, Allan Bieber, Kathleen Creager, Vicky Giordano, Molly Hair, Amaria Najem O'Leary, Patrick O'Leary, Marti Riley, and Jeffrey Witt — my faithful team of readers: *Thank you* for your dedication to reading my final drafts, you busy people! You're good! Your sharp focus and eloquent suggestions are woven into these pages. You have taught me that, although it appears to be a monologue, good preaching is really a dialogue with the community of faith.

To Kathleen Creager, my computer guru: *Thank you* for running the homestretch with me. It was a long one!

To the Sisters of Saint Francis at Assisi Heights in Rochester, Minnesota, and Luther College in Decorah, Iowa: *Thank you* for the quiet places to work.

To Gary, Betsy, Sarah, and Jake Dreier — my faithful family: *Thank you* for not only reading and improving these manuscripts, but for living with me through the process. As always, you are my support, my joy, and my true partners in faith. I'd promise life will get back to normal now, but I'm not sure what that is!

Again to Gary — my love: *Deepest thanks* for believing in me, especially when I don't.

God's Word is indeed the means of grace! Being immersed in these texts for many months has been life-giving to me. *Thanks and praise to you, O Lord!*

Table Of Contents

The Bus Driver

The Call Is Out!

"The kingdom of heaven may be compared to a king who gave a wedding banquet for his son" (Matthew 22:2).

Picture those invitations: gold-edged, hand-addressed by the royal calligrapher, each carrying the king's own seal. What an honor to be on that guest list!

The big day arrives. The lights in the kitchens have been on all night. The air is rich with the smells of roasting veal and baking bread. The weary night shift has gone home, and the excited day crew has arrived. Thousands of bouquets of flowers have been delivered. Dozens of long tables are set with white linens and silver place settings. The wine is poured, the candles are lit, and the wait staff in spotless uniforms stands ready to serve.

Finally the trumpets sound and the castle doors open ceremoniously for the invited guests. There is a collective gasp. No one is there! Something is terribly wrong.

The invited guests have "made light" (Matthew 22:5) of their invitations and thrown them aside — into drawers, garbage cans, or piles of unopened mail on their desks. No one is planning to come.

But the banquet is still ready and God, the host, won't give up until the seats are filled. The new call is out — and *everybody's* in! The slaves are sent out to round up anyone they can find, "both good and bad" (Matthew 22:10). This has become a "come-as-you-are" banquet.

9

With no entrance requirements, what a diverse list ends up in God's guest book! Here's the picture: business executives seated next to street people; inmates served the same feast as judges; gays and lesbians breaking bread with their straight neighbors; grease-encrusted hands brushing against well-manicured fingertips at the cake table.

As in the parable, the same call is out among us — and everybody's still in! God's guest list continues to be inclusive and diverse. Yet we are all seated at the same table, feasting on the same meal, guests of the same host — God. The differences in race, power, and social status, which seemed so important in our "old" lives, become less visible as God's grace, like a garment, covers us.

This is a "come-as-you-are-but-don't-stay-that-way" party! When we are given this wedding garment of new life and fed the bread and wine of God's grace, *we are changed!* Clothed in Christ (Galatians 3:27), a whole new self emerges (Colossians 3:10).

God's love transforms our lives, even as God sends us out to invite others to the celebration. At God's banquet there is a place marked with each of our names — with all names. The invitation is meant for everyone. The call is out! God's table must be filled!

The Bus Driver

The parable of the wedding party gives us a vision of the joyous and inclusive heavenly feast to come. It's also a pattern for *our lives* in anticipation of it. This is what God invites our *church gatherings* to look like!

Tom understood this. Tom was a big man with a big appetite. He not only loved to eat, he loved to cook. One of his favorite projects was baking all the bread for communion at his church. He would show up on Sunday mornings with his generous — and sometimes warm! — round loaves, a cross imprint baked into the crusty tops. He felt that the Lord's Supper, as a foretaste of the heavenly feast to come, should certainly have the best bread he could possibly bake! Using his bread baking to serve his church was one way Tom shared God's love with those around him.

Tom was a smart man who could have done many things with his life. He chose to use his intelligence and talents to be a bus driver. He was in his element when he settled into the driver's seat of his city bus each morning.

Everyone who stepped onto Tom's bus entered a unique little community on wheels traveling the streets of town. He welcomed everybody as they got on the bus, from the business executives to the street people, from the grease-covered to the well-groomed. One-time bus riders could immediately sense the friendliness on Tom's bus. Daily riders sat by old friends as they rode. And everybody chatted with Tom.

Tom was sure of one thing: God's love. His life had not always been easy, but God's love had brought him through many difficult times. When people unloaded their problems to him, he assured them of God's love for them. When people talked about the world's problems, he freely talked about the power of God's love to change things. And when people asked him about his "WWJD" bracelet, he routinely gave it to them as a reminder that God's actions always demonstrate God's love. He was always coming home needing another one.

Everyone was welcomed on Tom's bus. Everyone was welcome to experience God's love through Tom.

Good News Hits The Streets

And everyone was welcome to Tom's church.

When his church was drafting a new mission statement, Tom helped. He'd often challenge the other church members, "Say that in bus language. When people ask me what my church is like, I want to be able to give them our mission statement. I've got to have it in bus language." Tom knew that to extend God's invitation to the people on the streets, you have to talk their language.

And that's what he did. As he drove around town, he told people about his church. He eagerly invited them to come, as if he were inviting them to a magnificent feast — which, according to the parable, it is! On Sundays when the buses didn't run, he picked them up in his car to bring them to church. He was always going up to the pastors and saying, "I brought someone this morning I'd

11

like you to meet." Usually they were people he had met on his bus, people from all walks of life.

One cold fall day Tom called the church with a request. "Do you think we could find a winter coat somewhere for a woman who rides my bus?" She wore a very large size, and therefore couldn't find one at the Goodwill or Salvation Army stores. Minnesota winter was coming, and Tom was concerned. The church passed the word, and Tom's request was generously filled by someone in the congregation. Tom was able to give the woman a coat.

Tom was a present-day example of the servants in Jesus' parable who were sent out to fill the banquet hall.

When we share God's love through our words and our actions, we are sharing the invitation to God's banquet of grace. As Saint Francis once said, "Preach the gospel at all times; if necessary, use words."

The Church Where Anybody Can Come!

Somebody heard about Tom's church and said, "Oh, that's the church where anybody can come!" Tom and others made that a reality in their church, as they brought people of all races and economic backgrounds to worship.

Churches have many defining characteristics, but the wedding banquet in the Bible gives us a common, defining characteristic: each church is meant to be an *inviting* church. Use bus language, office language, school language, whatever language you need to spread this Good News and bring God's people to God's banquet!

God's banquet is set. There is a place marked with each of our names — and some people don't even know it. Like Tom driving the streets of town, God sends us out to pass this invitation by what we say and by what we do.

The parable of the wedding party gives us a vision of the joyous and inclusive heavenly feast to come. May it be the pattern for *our lives* in anticipation of it. And may our *church gatherings* be a welcome expression in the world of this extravagant grace of God.

The Wedding Dress

"Take my life, that I may be ..."

Laurie liked to play hymns on the piano and sing. She always started and finished with her favorite, "Take My Life That I May Be." And while she sang, she dreamed about the future. "Take my life that I may be consecrated, Lord, to thee...." What would she do with her life? She'd be lost in hopes as she continued, "Take my hands and let them move at the impulse of your love...."

But there was one line she never quite liked. "Take my silver and my gold, not a mite would I withhold...." It seemed a little out of touch with reality, that "not a mite" part. After all, you had to live in the world, didn't you? And it takes money. She wondered about her financial responsibilities as a Christian.

In the Bible the Pharisees tried to trick Jesus on this tough financial question, but Jesus gave a trick answer to their trick question! He said, "Give therefore to the emperor the things that are the emperor's, and to God the things that are God's."

And what is the emperor's that is not already God's? Ah, the Jews knew their Psalms. "The earth is the Lord's and all that is in it, the world, and those who live in it" (Psalm 24:1). "The heavens are yours, the earth also is yours; the world and all that is in it — you have founded them" (Psalm 89:11).

The rulers of the world claim a portion of our goods, but they do not own what is God's. Jesus could not be tricked into compartmentalizing God's reign into a separate, little box.

Yet, to the eavesdropping Roman ear, Jesus' answer was a perfectly equitable response: give what is due to each ruler.

13

It took Laurie a long time to understand what this means.

"Consecrated, Lord, to thee ..."

When Laurie graduated from college with an elementary education major, she took a one-year position as a teacher in a little village in Mexico. She had heard about poverty in Mexico — but nothing could have prepared her for this. The teachers' apartments were right next to the school, if you could call them apartments. The other teachers called them "huts with plumbing," but they were mansions compared to where her students lived.

When Laurie first walked through the door of her own "hut," tears stung her eyes. What was she doing here? What was she thinking? Many of her friends had already "gotten settled" into comfortable American schools, with adequate incomes and nice apartments. They wouldn't think of going without a curling iron for a whole year, much less a coffee maker! How was she going to survive, hundreds of miles from everyone she loved and everything she knew?

"Take my moments and my days ..."

There was a timid knock at her door. Several school-age children crowded into the doorway to get a peek at the new teacher.

Within a few weeks, those knocks at the door became daily occurrences. Late afternoon and early evening, the children would come — to visit, for help with schoolwork, and often just to be there. She didn't mind the extra time spent with them. She was already starting to love these kids, their families, and this little village.

Laurie's few possessions were like treasures to them. They held her unlit candles gently in their laps, memorized all the faces in her family portrait, and paged through her paperbacks as if they were able to read them. It was fun to see how her "stuff" delighted them.

Laurie surveyed her homey little apartment. She had packed light for the year, but now many of these "bare necessities" she had brought seemed *unnecessary* — even extravagant. (And then there's that small mountain of boxes and bins stored in her parents' basement!).

"Take my silver and my gold ..."

She had given up a lot — especially income — to come here this year. (She began to wonder what on earth she would have *done* with all that income.) She asked God how to use her wealth in the middle of so much poverty. For the first time, it dawned on her that an understanding of "Take my silver and my gold ..." began with the heart.

There was one thing she never let the children see. At least once a week, late at night when she was all alone, she pulled it out of the back of her closet: her graduation dress, a gift from her parents. It was the nicest dress she'd ever owned, but it was so much more than that: it was the pride of graduation, and great college memories, and home, and her parents' love — all in that one special dress. It somehow brought her family closer to her, and when she was lonely it reminded her how special she was to them.

"Not a mite would I withhold ..."

One day, in early spring, Maria knocked on her door. Maria had never before come to Laurie's, although her younger brothers and sisters were there often. Maria was in her teens and worked at the clothing factory in the nearby town. Her income fed the entire family.

Maria's eyes sparkled. She was getting married, in just two months. Laurie hugged her and congratulated her. Then Maria, head bowed, quietly asked Laurie for help. She had brought over a well-worn old dress and a white shawl, and wondered if Laurie could help her sew something special from them for the wedding.

Laurie held up the old garments, and tried to think of something they could design from them. Back home, she'd packed up clothes to Salvation Army that were far nicer than these. She told Maria they'd try, and Maria should come back Saturday to work on it.

That night she felt particularly lonely. Her college roommate had gotten married the day after graduation, and here she was in Mexico alone, unattached, and no one waiting back home for her. So, of course, she reached into the back of her closet for her dress.

15

She hugged it to herself and cried softly, so aware of her emptiness in the middle of her little "Mexican adventure."

As she gently placed it back into the closet, those nagging words popped into her head. "Take my silver and my gold, not a mite would I withhold...." She pulled the dress back out and eyed it carefully. Yes, it was the right shade. Yes, it was close to the right size. Yes, it could be temporarily hemmed. Yes, it would be a perfect dress for Maria to use on her wedding day.

Laurie thought of the Psalm that says, "The earth is the Lord's and everything in it...." It started to make sense to her that, if *everything* is God's, then what we have is "on loan" from God, to be gratefully received and generously used. What was "on loan" to her from God could be "on loan" from her to Maria.

Letting Maria use her prized possession as a wedding dress suddenly felt like an *honor* to Laurie. She couldn't wait for Saturday, and the surprise she had for Maria. "Not a mite would I withhold...." It was a matter of the heart.

Money For Caesar ...

"Give therefore to the emperor the things that are the emperor's ..." (Matthew 22:21a).

We live simultaneously in God's realm and the human realm, and Jesus calls us to responsibility in both. Go ahead: pay your state sales tax, license your cars, and file an honest tax return. Give to the government whatever it takes to conduct its business. But remember: our *things* as well as *ourselves* belong to God, and are here for God's purposes to be accomplished.

This is good news for a culture tyrannized by acquisition and materialism. These "things" that consume so much of us are *not* what life is about at all. We are part of something larger than this life. We are part of the kingdom of God, where we matter for who we are and not for what we have accomplished or acquired.

Hearts For God

"... and (give) to God the things that are God's" (Matthew 25:21b).

Jesus invites us to be free of the tyranny of our possessions, "for where your treasure is, there your heart will be also" (Matthew 6:21). When we take this truth to heart, we can begin to separate our needs from our greeds and become caretakers rather than consumers. Stewardship replaces accumulation, and our possessions become a means to an end rather than the end itself.

"Not a mite would I withhold...." Jesus Christ withheld nothing when "he emptied himself and took on the form of a servant ... (to) death on a cross" (Philippians 2:7-8). It is God's way, and now it becomes our way as well.

Laurie joined in the village celebration of Maria and Carlos' wedding two months later, and she was not nervous at all about her dress. From now on, every time she pulled it out from the back of her closet, it would carry even more memories than before. Now it tied together her two worlds, home and Mexico, and the love she felt in both.

We cannot really give to God what is already God's. But we can release ourselves and our possessions to God's purposes. It's a matter of the heart.

Proper 25
Pentecost 23
Ordinary Time 30
Matthew 22:34-46

Faith Hardware

To hang a cabinet door, you need two hinges. Like a door, our faith hangs from two hinges: love of God and love of humanity. Jesus said:

> " 'You shall love the Lord your God with all your heart, and with all your soul, and with all your mind.' This is the greatest and first commandment. And a second is like it: 'You shall love your neighbor as yourself.' On these two commandments hang all the law and the prophets" (Matthew 22:37-40).

These two commandments sum up all the commandments in the Bible, including the Ten Commandments. They connect us to God and each other, and both are vital to the life of faith. We might say these two hinges are the hardware of faith.

Hinge One: Love God

Jillian Larson lived the life most young people wish they had. Her parents loved her; her sister Karen was her best friend; they lived in the exclusive Brookside Terrace with many other physicians' families; she was personable and attractive; she made National Merit Finalist; even her tennis game was looking up.

People thought Jillian "had it all," but there was a hole in her life. Early in her teen years she began to believe that she needed a boyfriend in order to be happy. What started out as a cute "want" in middle school evolved into an obsession in high school. She watched as her friends dated, and jokingly named herself the "perpetually-single best friend" to all the girls who had boyfriends. She pretended it didn't bother her that things never worked out between her and guys.

In her heart it was much more than a joke. Her desire for a boyfriend gradually turned into other issues. She was always down on herself. Maybe if she were skinnier, maybe if she had better clothes, maybe if she could "party hearty," then she'd find the right guy. She hated herself for eating, she spent an amazing amount of money on clothes, and she tried to prove at parties that she could be bad enough to be dated. Everything she did, she did with the hope that somehow it would help her meet that man of her dreams.

It's not that she really lacked love in her life. She knew she was loved by God and her family and even her friends. This was different. She prayed for God's help. She prayed every night for a boyfriend. Each day she'd look for the answer to her prayers, but it never came. *He* never came.

The renewal notice arrived for her subscription to a teen fashion magazine. The notice said, "How are you going to know the hottest new fashions, how are you going to be popular and know how to get the hot boys without your subscription? Renew your favorite magazine for another year!" She crammed it into her backpack and headed out the door for a church youth retreat.

The theme for the retreat weekend was "God's Awesome Love." She'd heard it all before, but this weekend was different. For some reason, it really sunk in. God loved *her!* This truth came to life for her, as if she were hearing it for the very first time.

For years she had been thinking about finding a boyfriend, finding that first taste of romance, finding love. She had been desperately looking for a perfect love, and confusing her spiritual needs with her desire for a boyfriend. Now she realized that while she searched, God's love was — and had always been — right in front of her.

Jesus died for *her!* It was this unconditional love that she really craved — the love that would never break up with her, reject her, or make her feel insecure. Yes, she still wanted a boyfriend, but God's love was the love that she truly couldn't live without.

She began to feel strangely free — free to relax and be herself, secure in God's love for her.

The retreat leader challenged them to find a way to respond to God's awesome love. Jillian reached into her backpack and tore up the magazine renewal notice. She'd been subscribing for too long to *that* path for love!

Jillian had been preoccupied with having a boyfriend, and had let that become the most important thing on her mind and in her heart. It had spread like cancer into other parts of her life, taking over more and more. Jesus said, " 'You shall love the Lord your God with all your heart, and with all your soul, and with all your mind' " (Matthew 22:37). This is the greatest and first commandment. It releases us from the bondage of our world, and the things that ultimately disappoint us, let us down, and even consume us.

What matters most to you? Think about your own life and what's most important to you. God invites us to let go of whatever is taking God's place in our hearts and souls and minds.

Like a hinge on a door, this commandment connects us securely to the love of God, and frees us to live as God intended. It keeps our lives from coming "unhinged" from the one love that gives us life!

Hinge Two: Love Humanity

Thuy Linh had been the nanny and housekeeper in Jillian's home for fifteen years. Every morning before dawn she rode the bus across town to the exclusive neighborhood where the Larsons lived, arriving in time for the Larson parents to get to their respective offices.

Jillian and her sister Karen had known Thuy Linh since they were preschoolers, and had grown up calling her "Mama T." She liked that, even though her own children were unquestionably the center of her life. Jillian and Karen would rather not think about Mama T having her own life and her own children, because they adored her so. Even now, as sophisticated high schoolers, they looked forward to after-school snack time with Mama T before they headed off to tennis lessons or to play practice.

Dr. Mary Larson, their mother, felt lucky that Mama T was always there for the girls. Their father, "JW" Larson, a local business owner, was pleased with the consistency Mama T provided the girls in the middle of their busy lifestyle.

The large church in town had a special outreach to Vietnamese people. Mama T and her family attended worship every Sunday in the gym while the Larson family worshiped in the sanctuary.

It was Lent. Maundy Thursday worship services were going to be combined this year — the Vietnamese congregation and the "regular" congregation worshiping together in the gym. Footwashing was a big part of the Maundy Thursday service in the church. As Dr. Mary Larson knelt before one of the chairs, she was startled to find Mama T seated before her.

As she washed Mama T's feet, she noticed deep scars across her left ankle and extending up her leg. How could she have never noticed them before? Ugly wounds had healed unevenly, leaving deep ripples of scarred skin in jagged folds. She had heard that Thuy Linh and her family had narrowly escaped from Vietnam, but she had never thought ...

The evidence of these wounds stunned her. She hesitated, and glanced up at Mama T. With her characteristic warmth, Mama T nodded for Mary to proceed. It was okay to touch her feet; the pain was years in the past.

As Mary washed Mama T's feet, she stroked them gently. And then the tears began. How could someone have done this to another human being? And how could *she* have never noticed before? She bowed her head so her long hair would hide her tears, but they rolled off her cheeks and onto Mama T's feet.

Over the years Mama T had given untold hours of care to Jillian and Karen, and yet Mary had shown only professional courtesies to Mama T herself. As Dr. Mary Larson knelt there on the floor of the church gymnasium, her hair soaked with tears, she felt a mixture of love and gratitude for this dear woman seated before her.

Dr. Mary Larson had been so preoccupied with her own life, that she had completely overlooked another human being right in her own household. Jesus said, " 'You shall love your neighbor as yourself' " (Matthew 22:39). God's love breaks down the isolation of individualism, and unites us with each other.

That day a change began to happen in the Larson home. The professional contract Mary and JW Larson had *for* Mama T's services became a relationship *with* Mama T and the household became more like a family.

Think about all the people in your life, ranging from family members to casual acquaintances to the general public. God invites us to a *lifestyle* of relationships, showing love to our sister and brother human beings as we love ourselves.

There is an implied template for behavior in Jesus' words. He assumes we treat ourselves well and with respect, so he urges us to treat our neighbor as ourselves. Valuing the preciousness of humanity goes both ways, as healthy self-love and self-respect move out from ourselves to others.

Like a hinge on a door, this commandment connects us securely to human love. It keeps our lives from coming "unhinged" from the relationships with others that flesh out God's loving purposes for us.

Two Hinges Of Faith

Want to know how to love God? Open your heart and soul and mind to God. Like young Jillian, see what's most important there and let go of whatever is replacing God's reign in your life.

Want to know how to love your neighbor? Open yourself to other people. Like Mary Larson, discover our common bond of humanity and begin to share the love which unites us equally under God's love.

Which is most important?

Prioritizing the Law has been fodder for debates for more than two millennia. It was one of the issues that the Pharisees raised with Jesus, hoping to snag him on the complexities of the question.

But Jesus brought an age-old debate into sharp focus for all time. What's more important: loving God or loving neighbor? The answer is: both. "On these two commandments hang all the law and the prophets," said Jesus (Matthew 22:40).

Jesus saw them as two hinges on the same door. Everything hangs from both of them, and therefore both are vital to a vibrant faith. God's love, given and received, is our faith hardware.

May it keep us "hinged" in grace and abundant life.

Proper 26
Pentecost 24
Ordinary Time 31
Matthew 23:1-12

Serving Faith

Pharisees Today

The Pharisees were real "good news/bad news" guys!

They were the undisputed authorities on the Jewish Scriptures, and the recognized spokespersons for Moses himself. "Do whatever they teach you and follow it," Jesus said to the crowds and to his disciples (Matthew 23:3a). We hear so much about Jesus in conflict with the Pharisees, that sometimes we forget Jesus respectfully acknowledged their academic accomplishments and religious leadership.

But the old cliché was true about them: they only "talked the talk" and didn't "walk the walk." Jesus bluntly continued, "But do not do as they do, for they do not practice what they teach" (Matthew 23:3b). They had fallen into the age-old human trap of enjoying the honor and admiration of others, and forgetting that faith is *active* as well as *academic*.

It's a trap people still fall into today.

Melanie is the kind of person the Pharisees and scribes were in Jesus' day. She is deeply religious. She knows her Bible well, and is quick to talk about Jesus to her friends at work and school.

She's definitely admirable. When people think about someone with great faith, they think of Melanie. She's forceful and eloquent about her beliefs and when she speaks, people listen.

But there's a problem. She *lifts up* her faith in a manner that leaves the people around her feeling generally *put down*. There's no question that her dedication to God is real, but she wears it like a personal badge of honor that sets her apart from others.

25

She's at church meetings and Bible studies several times a week, but never has time to serve on a committee or help her church serve dinner at the Dorothy Day House or serve even one year as a Sunday school teacher. The word "serve" just isn't part of her faith.

If a friend has a problem, Melanie doesn't really take the time to listen or be supportive. Yet she's quick with advice, and always sure she's right. About faith. About everything. It's hard to put a finger on it, but even though Melanie talks a lot about Jesus, her faith seems to point as much to Melanie herself as to Jesus.

The Flu

The point of our faith is to point to Jesus. Sometimes we get so impressed with ourselves, like the Pharisees and Melanie, that we seem to forget there is just one God. As Jesus instructed his disciples, even our religious strivings can deceive us; there is but one teacher (23:8), one Father in heaven (23:9), one Messiah (23:10).

And there is but one true servant. Jesus says, "The greatest among you will be your servant." He was foreshadowing his way to the cross, and opening up our way to follow.

We need to set aside the idea of achieving our own greatness, if we are to follow Jesus into servanthood. If we *try* to be great, we're on the wrong path. If we try to be great through servanthood, our *serving* becomes *self-serving*. Then we've lost the very idea of service.

Once in awhile we meet someone who really seems to understand true servanthood. Louise is one of these people.

Louise is deeply religious, and quietly faithful at attending church and church functions. Sometimes people don't even notice she's there, because she might be in the back of the sanctuary walking a baby for a frazzled mother or in the kitchen getting the refreshments ready.

She's not very sure of herself in Bible studies because she can't always remember Bible passages like Melanie can. However God is very real to her, and she knows that she wouldn't make it through each day without faith.

26

She's loved by many. When people think of someone they could turn to in a time of need, they think of Louise. And sometimes they don't even have to ask.

One Saturday Louise's friend Norma had the flu, and so did Norma's husband Joe and their young children. All at the same time. Norma and Joe were changing bedding, soothing fevered little ones, wiping up floors, and frequently stopping at the bathroom themselves. It was a nightmare.

Out of the blue, Louise called just to see how Norma was and to chat. When Norma told Louise they all had the flu, Louise said, "I'll be right over." Norma protested, telling Louise to stay away because things were *really bad*. Louise said again, "I'll be right over." And then she hung up.

Louise came right over to Norma's house. She spent the rest of the day scrubbing floors, making and serving jello, and washing clothes and bedding. Norma and Joe rested. By the time Louise went home that evening, Norma and Joe were feeling well enough to take care of things again, and the house was back in order.

Norma didn't see or hear from Louise for about a week after that. One day Norma was talking to a mutual friend and asked about Louise. "Oh, haven't you heard? She came down with a terrible flu bug a few days ago. Worst she's ever had. She's a little weak, but she's doing better now."

Norma felt awful. She called Louise right away to apologize, because it was clear Louise had gotten the flu by helping her and Joe. Louise just laughed. "Well, I s'pose that's what comes from hanging around sick people!" she joked. And all Norma could say was, "Thank you."

Louise will never be written up in *People* magazine for it, but she performed a true act of greatness that day by serving Norma and Joe. She pointed to Jesus without saying a word.

The Way Of The Cross
The point of faith is to point to Jesus. The famous Isenheim Altarpiece is a magnificent, multiple-paneled painting of the story of faith done by Mathias Grunewald in the early 1500s. The outside panel shows the overwhelming agony of Jesus on the cross.

Next to him is John the Baptist, pointing his disproportionately large index finger to Jesus. On the canvas are painted John's words, "He must increase but I must decrease" (John 3:30).

Our serving points to Christ, like the long index finger of John the Baptist in Grunewald's painting. The best we can do is let Christ be great through us. Greatness is grace!

Melanie's faith, though admirable, stopped short of service. Jesus' ministry of servanthood continues in the gritty, "down and dirty," day-to-day tasks like Louise did for Norma and Joe when they had the flu. It's not always pretty. Sometimes we pay a price for servanthood, as Louise did when she got sick, as Jesus did when he died on the cross.

Paradoxically, the way of the cross *is* the way to life. It is the path Jesus opened up to us. It is God's way. And in the power of the resurrection, in God's time, "those who humble themselves will be exalted" (Matthew 23:12).

Let It Shine

Jesus told a story about ten bridesmaids whose job it was to bring wedding torches to shine for the arrival of the bridegroom. Five of them ran out of fuel. Let's imagine the story from the perspective of one of the foolish bridesmaids who didn't have enough fuel for her torch. Her story might go something like this:

Anna's Story, Part 1

"My name is Anna, one of the five 'foolish' bridesmaids. Right off the bat, I'd like to clear up one thing: we *did* bring *some* oil that night! We weren't foolish enough to bring our torches without any oil at all, because our lights were burning for a while. But we didn't bring an emergency supply, and the wait for the groom was much longer than anyone expected. I mean, it was *midnight* before the wedding party arrived!

"When my friends asked me to be a bridesmaid in their wedding, I was so excited! I wanted to be the best bridesmaid ever! We had a year to get ready. I started right away planning an engagement party, giving a shower, making their present, and going on lots of shopping trips. I had so many lists, no one could say I didn't care about being prepared.

"In hindsight, I'd have to say I lost my focus over the year. I was trying so hard to be a good bridesmaid that I got too busy with too many things. The bottom line is this: the wedding night came, and my light went out. That was the most important thing I had to do, and I foolishly neglected it by not having extra oil along. The

29

next day I checked my things-to-do list titled, 'The Big Day.' Extra oil was the only thing *not* crossed off.

"Ironically, I didn't even *need* the extra pair of shoes I put in my backpack for the torch dance. The torch dance is a special dance the bridesmaids do when the groom arrives, and I missed it all.[1] By the time we got back from buying oil, we were even too late to get into the banquet. They didn't even recognize us as the bridesmaids, I guess because bridesmaids are supposed to be there early with their torches and not show up late begging to get in.

"Jesus told our story to illustrate how the kingdom of heaven might come later than we think, but we should be prepared. Faith is like our torches, and we need to be sure we have plenty of fuel to keep the light burning even if it's a very long wait. As time went on, I got sidetracked. I was so busy trying to be the best bridesmaid around, that I messed up on the basic job of tending my torch. Jesus sure made his point by telling our story."

Anna's Story, Part 2

"Lots of people are like us five foolish bridesmaids. The funny thing is, we each made *different* foolish mistakes, that let our lights go out.

"As I said, my light went out because I got sidetracked. It's easy to get 'faith sidetracked' by doing all kinds of religious stuff thinking we can impress God and be the best Christian around, but forgetting to 'keep the main thing the *main thing*.'

"Another bridesmaid, my friend Deborah, ran out of money. She got her nails done and her hair highlighted and even bought a fancy little purse that matched our dresses — things that really didn't matter. She didn't have anything left to buy oil, so her light went out, too. Some people spend their lives on things that don't matter, but don't invest anything in keeping their faith light going.

"And Lois just ran out of time. She'd been meaning to pick up extra oil, but never got around to it. Her intentions were good, but that didn't keep her light going. I know some people do the same with faith, figuring they'll worry about God and religion later. That's what my dad thought, except he ran out of time and died of a heart attack.

"Then there's Rhoda. She was never a Girl Scout because she hates that motto: 'Be Prepared.' She'd rather take risks than play it safe, which is why she *decided* not to bring extra oil. But her light went out, just like the rest of ours. Some people think faith is a crutch for weaklings who can't stand on their own in this risky world. They get more and more self-confident and start thinking nothing will ever happen to them.

"Poor Martha put some extra oil in a bottle on the shelf months before the wedding and then, because that little detail was taken care of, she forgot about it. Then, of course, she didn't have it when her oil ran low, and her light went out. Some people think they just have to do a few things to put faith 'in order,' like they're taking out an insurance policy for heaven. Then they set it aside and forget about it.

"In the end, what matters is whether our 'faith light' is shining for the Lord and showing the way for others. With each of us, it didn't. Our lights went out.

"They tell me the torch dance that night was dim and disappointing, since only half of the bridesmaids were there to dance with their lights. At the wedding banquet, our five places at the head table were empty, like we'd died or something. My friends, the bride and groom, were sad about how things turned out. So were we."

"Let it shine, let it shine, let it shine!"

These are five fictitious stories based on Jesus' parable. They illustrate just some of the ways people can end up without enough fuel to keep their faith lights burning. So the question is, "How's your light doing?"

The question is an important one. There is an undeniably ominous ending to Jesus' parable: the five foolish bridesmaids are gone to get oil when the festivities begin, and consequently are excluded from the wedding feast. But this story is not about just making it through the door of the heavenly banquet. It is an invitation to the torch dance of life that leads to fulfillment in the wedding feast to come.

We do not have to create our own flame of faith, like cold campers rubbing stones together to ignite a small spark. It has been given to us.

The torch of faith is passed on to us in baptism. As God lights the faith fire, the church lights a baptism candle and symbolically hands it off to us with the words, "Let your light shine before others, so that they may see your good works and give glory to your Father in heaven" (Matthew 5:16). This directive to let our lights shine, placed early in Matthew's Gospel, helps set the context for the failure of the five bridesmaids to keep their lights burning.

Our job is to tend the faith flame and keep it burning. Pray. Read your Bible. Be part of a worshiping Christian community. These are fuel for the fire.

Jesus' story makes it clear that being included in God's kingdom can't happen on someone else's preparations. The five unprepared bridesmaids couldn't borrow oil from the five who were prepared with enough oil. Neither can we live off someone else's flame. The five unprepared bridesmaids had to go buy oil because they needed to have *their* torches burning. We have to participate with our own flame — tending it, fueling it and, of course, shining it.

But what happens to the enthusiasm of the children singing with all their hearts, "This little light of mine, I'm gonna let it shine"? And what happens to our enthusiasm for the gospel as we plod along in life? And what of the long wait when, in our weariness, we cry with the psalmist, "How long, O Lord? How long?"

Jesus' parable sparks our imaginations again. Imagine the brightness! Imagine the excitement when finally the long-awaited news comes, " 'Here is the bridegroom! Come out to meet him!' " (Matthew 25:6). Imagine the joy of the torch dance, the feasting at the wedding banquet!

Our mission in the world with each of our lamps is simple but vital: "let it shine, let it shine, let it shine."

Shining Together

The light of each individual is crucial. But when combined with the lights of others, they shine much more powerfully.

32

Many years ago, there was a small village that had no church. Except for one wealthy landowner, most of the people in this village were poor and struggling. The wealthy man came to the village council with a proposal: He would like to build a church for the village. He would personally fund the whole project. The only condition he placed on them was this: He must be *completely* in charge of the project, down to every little detail. They were somewhat reluctant to have no say at all in the project, but they could hardly turn down such a generous offer. They agreed to his proposal and his conditions.

The villagers watched with curiosity as construction began. They were amazed at the size of the foundation, impressed with the fine quality materials being used, and generally very excited. And there were some who were frustrated about being left out of the decisions. He must need their input about *something*. They were sure he'd forget something vital.

Finally the construction was done, and the day came for the villagers to step inside their church. They were in awe. It was truly magnificent! A few, of course, were sure they'd discover something wrong somewhere, something forgotten. Finally someone discovered, "There are no lights in this whole place!" It was true; there were absolutely no lights mounted anywhere in the mammoth sanctuary.

The man just smiled and pointed up. There was a continuous row of pegs on the walls around the whole inside of the church. Each peg had the name of a villager engraved beneath it.

He passed out a lantern to each villager, from the month-old infant to the elderly. "When you come to worship, you must bring your lantern and place it on your peg. When you are here, all of our lives will be brighter. When you *all* come, the whole church will be brilliantly lit. But when you do not come, the church — and each of our lives — will be that much dimmer."

And so we fuel our lights and carry God's flame with us wherever we go. Anna and Deborah, Lois, Rhoda, and Martha, we need you! Each light matters.

Individually, our lights provide a unique brightness in the world as we wait for this joyful fulfillment of God's promises. Joined together as the church, our lights become stronger and brighter than we could ever be alone in this sin-darkened world.

The air is filled with excitement, not terror, when we are ready with our hearts and our lamps burning to see Jesus. We wait with anticipation for the promised announcement, "Here is the bridegroom! Come!"

May we be wise and watchful, faithful and focused, that the light of Christ we bear in the world may grow brighter and not dim as time waits for eternity.

---

1. Eduard Schweizer, *The Good News According To Matthew*, trans. David E. Green (Atlanta: John Knox Press, 1975), pp. 465-466.

Dance, Rosa, Dance

Rosa's Gift

Rosa checked the list again. Maybe she had just missed her name. Her eyes searched from top to bottom, but it was not there. So why had she come here, so far away from home, if she didn't make Dance Troupe? The Theatre/Dance Department was why she chose this college! She might just as well pack up and go home.

Then she noticed another list titled "Ensemble of Dance." There was her name. She would get to dance — but in the group for *beginners*. She felt such a mixture of feelings: yes, it was a chance to dance, but, no, it was not the highly-regarded Dance Troupe.

She had a gift for dance. She had been told that her whole life. She knew it deep inside herself. At least weekly she danced in her dreams. Sometimes she'd wake up so tangled in her sheets and blankets, she had to re-make her bed in the middle of the night. She prayed often about her gift, wondering why God had given it to her, wanting to give glory to God — and not sure how.

That night she prayed for guidance. She felt God had led her here but this was a real blow to her plans. She felt like quitting and only one thing kept her going: she knew that God had given her this gift for dance, and she was certain of her calling to use it.

She swallowed her pride and threw herself into the Ensemble of Dance. She also signed up for dance lessons and general music lessons. She decided that even if she weren't as accomplished as others, she'd at least be using the gift God gave her.

Mid-year she took the risk and again tried out for the Dance Troupe, but again didn't make it. That was really hard to take, and

35

she wondered what God was doing! She spent even longer hours practicing for her dance and music lessons, frustrated and yet more determined than ever.

That summer she got a job as a resident recreation leader at a children's home. She was so busy she couldn't practice dance as she had intended. But something else happened: she discovered the children liked to dance too. She playfully danced with them. She made up games using dance steps, and even helped some of them put on a little dance show. She really felt God was helping her reach out to these children through dance.

And once a week, she had to get up in the middle of the night and re-make her bed because she was tangled in the sheets while "dream dancing." She felt like God just wouldn't let her ignore her gift.

Dancing so much with the children, her own ability actually improved over the summer. When she got to campus that fall, she auditioned again for the Dance Troupe. She prayed again to get in, as she had done so often before, and yet she somehow felt more peaceful this time. Maybe she wouldn't ever make Dance Troupe, but she would definitely keep on dancing wherever God led her. She was sure of that, after using her dance ability in such surprising ways all summer.

They posted the list and she checked for her name. Again. And again. Three times she read it to make sure. Yes, that *was* her name, right near the top of the list! She prayed, "Thank you, God!" even before the tears welled up in her eyes.

Rosa's story serves as a contrast to the third servant in the parable of the talents, who was given charge of some of his master's property and did nothing but bury it. A year earlier Rosa had been tempted to bury her gift and forget it, like the servant in the parable.

Instead she kept believing in dance as a gift to her from God. She used her gift, developed it, and kept going in spite of disappointments. Working at the children's home, she discovered the joy of *serving* with dance. It was only when she made Dance Troupe that she realized her skill had improved tremendously.

36

The parable calls each of us to serve God through the gifts given to us, trusting God to make productive use of our efforts for the kingdom.

Simple Gifts

The slaves in the parable of the talents receive dramatically different amounts of the master's property, but *even the smallest amount was still immensely valuable* in the currency of Jesus' time. Similarly, all that God has entrusted to us is valuable. After all, any gift from God is precious indeed.

Don't be fooled into thinking you have no gifts, for you are God's creation. God's gifts reside in everyone and, like seeds, are full of potential. Unfortunately it is almost routine for Christians to excuse themselves from work in the kingdom by protesting that their gifts, if they have any, are too modest to be significant.

Certainly there are people who stand out more than others because of their gifts: Dr. Martin Luther King, Jr., as a great leader, Mother Teresa as a remarkable servant, and Billy Graham as a dynamic preacher. As these people used their gifts, the world took note and was blessed through them.

Most of us, however, are ordinary people with simple gifts. According to Jesus' parable, even the modest gift is significant in the kingdom — a privilege with responsibility.

Like muscles that need to be worked or they wither, God's gifts can never be passively possessed. In the parable, the unproductive servant loses everything. Our differing gifts have been wisely given by God to use and develop, but not to bury.

Picture children on Christmas. Their enthusiasm is unbounded. Tear open the plastic wrap! Put the batteries in! Run the toy *now*! Children are not content to set gifts aside and passively enjoy them in the package. Their response is active: *use the gifts! Do what they're designed to do!*

That's the kind of enthusiasm for God's gifts that the parable encourages. Don't just maintain them or bury them safely in a hole in the ground. Use them! Risk a little! Otherwise they — and *we* — are worthless to the kingdom.

The Turning Point

Rosa's summer work at the children's home was a turning point for her. When she discovered she could serve others through her gift for dance, it took on new meaning and joy for her. *It was part of her calling to serve God.* In scriptures God similarly calls each of us to serve: "Like good stewards of the manifold grace of God, serve one another with whatever gift each of you has received" (1 Peter 4:10).

Our responsibility goes beyond ourselves. This parable takes aim at our tendency to live for our own goals and dedicate our efforts to our own comfort or security. We are part of something much larger than ourselves: the glorious kingdom of God. Our gifts have been given to us so that we might serve well in God's kingdom.

This is an important turning point for each of us. It isn't enough to acknowledge, use, and develop our gifts. We were made to find joy serving in God's kingdom. Our lives take on deeper meaning when our gifts lead us to servanthood, our blessings deepen our discipleship, and our purposes become God's purposes.

There's a wonderful old hymn which anchors our gifts in their Source, God:

> *We give thee but thine own*
> *Whate'er the gift may be;*
> *All that we have is thine alone,*
> *A trust, O Lord, from thee.*

A "trust" is property held for the benefit of another. Our gifts, of whatever magnitude, are "entrusted" to us by God for the benefit of God's kingdom. Our calling is to tend God's gifts as we attend to God's kingdom, never forgetting whose talents they are — God's — and whose purposes they serve — God's — and whose kingdom we await — again, God's.

The Promise

Rosa often wondered why God had given her this gift and she asked God for guidance in using it. She suffered many set-backs.

Through her journey of prayer and hard work, however, she began to see God's hand leading her and discovered the joy of serving through dance.

In the years ahead Rosa would continue to travel this road of prayer and hard work, looking often for God's guidance. Such is the journey of faith. It is a journey of utter freedom — not freedom from hard work, practice, and doing our best, but freedom from worrying about the outcome. *God* is at work through us.

God promises to help us. Like sprouting seeds, God's word "shall not return to me empty, but it shall accomplish that which I purpose," says the Lord (Isaiah 55:11).

"Therefore, my beloved, be steadfast, immovable, always excelling in the work of the Lord, because you know that in the Lord your labor is not in vain" (1 Corinthians 15:58).

Living in these promises, let us work faithfully for God's purposes. May we have the courage to invest ourselves and our gifts in the kingdom for which Jesus gave his life — and for which we have been given ours.

In The Meantime ...

The End Of The World?

There are many who fear the end of the world and the catastrophes they believe will accompany it.

It's no wonder some people suspected we were experiencing "the beginning of the end" when they turned on the evening news October 17, 1989. That was the day a devastating earthquake shook the San Francisco area, tossing life around as if in a blender. People braced themselves for more than aftershocks.

Throughout much of human history there have been people running about with alarming predictions of the end of the world, and surprising numbers of people have gotten caught up in their claims of impending disaster and doom.

It has intensified in our time, at the end of an old and beginning of a new millennium. Christian fundamentalists and apocalyptic fringe groups make prophecies with increasing intensity. Our human capacity to destroy ourselves through such things as a nuclear apocalypse or global warming has added a secular dimension to this end-of-the-world fever.

A surprising forty to sixty percent of Americans surveyed in the 1990s had a sense of doomsday coming soon.[1] People look with increasing suspicion at catastrophes like famine, war, AIDS, world hunger, chemical weapons, floods, and earthquakes.

Children have picked up on all this hovering fear, appropriating it into their personal encounters with calamity. Ten-year-old Andrew is one such example. He actually braced himself for the second coming of Jesus whenever a spring storm or tornado warning sent him

41

and his family into the basement. It was loud. It was scary. And he prayed fearfully, worried that the end of the world was coming and afraid he wouldn't go to heaven.

We seem to forget that a long time ago Jesus told us not to be alarmed about these things. Earthly calamities are an inevitable part of this world's struggles, but "the end is not yet" (Matthew 24:6). Jesus assures us not to look to these catastrophes as the signs of the end. They are just the early twinges of the contractions that will eventually give birth to the new age.

Yet fear grips us and global calamities are not the only things that shake us up. Sometimes it takes just a sentence and our whole world is shaken. "The biopsy report came back positive for melanoma." "Ma'am, your husband's been in a terrible accident." Or a child hearing, "Daddy isn't going to live here anymore."

Whether personal or global, sometimes the earth shakes under our feet. When the world as we know it begins to come apart, Jesus says, "Don't be alarmed." Whether we fear the end-times or our own end or the end of things we hold dear, Jesus' words comfort us. This world is still God's, and things are not out of control. We are anchored in spite of life's storms.

Jesus redirects us. There is something far more threatening to concern us than the end-times, catastrophes, and calamities. It is the evil that exists in the world all around us.

The Real Problem

Stephen Biko, a black South African, experienced that evil. He was a leader and spokesperson for his people in the 1970s. Apartheid was flattening black homelands in the name of "public health," imprisoning black leaders in the name of "public safety," and preventing black opportunity in the name of "the public good."

White leaders said Biko's death in prison in 1977 was due to a hunger strike and his own refusal of intravenous nutrition. His badly beaten corpse, secretly photographed, showed otherwise.

One powerful person knew the truth: a white South African newspaper editor named Donald Woods. (The movie *Cry Freedom* dramatized his true-life story.) Woods' knowledge led him to challenge the apartheid system.

42

He, too, became vulnerable to apartheid's cruel self-preservation tactics. Banned from publishing, traveling, or meeting with more than one person at a time, Woods wrote a book exposing the truth. He'd have to leave South Africa to get the message out to the world, and he'd have to take his family with him.

Donald's wife Wendy, supportive up to that point, opposed his plan to depart the country. Wendy was unwilling to rip their five children from their schools, grandparents, and the only home they'd ever known. This was taking the cause too far, as she saw it.

Then a package was delivered to their home, anonymously addressed to the Woods children. It contained T-shirts bearing the face of Stephen Biko. Excitedly they scrambled to put them on, but they began screaming immediately. Those shirts, treated with some kind of chemical, instantly began to burn the skin right off the children's hands and arms and faces.

At that moment, it was as if Wendy heard more than the horrifying screams of her own children. It was as if she heard, through them, the agonizing screams of black children throughout South Africa's homelands — screams of pain, of injustice, of horror. Whoever would do this to innocent children must be stopped.

The package was traced to the local security police. That night, as Wendy and Donald put their burned and bandaged children to bed, Wendy told Donald, "I think that book should be published." The horrible truths must be told. The horror must stop. They embarked upon a dangerous plan to escape South Africa to publish the book.

In South Africa hatred had become well-organized and institutionalized.

Most of the time it's much more subtle than that. Jesus warns us that while we wait for God's final fulfillment, we live in a world of decaying love that can be seen in human cruelty to other humans. Matthew 24 lists signs of this evil: torture, killings, and hatred (v. 10); deceit (v. 11); lawlessness and love grown cold (v. 12). These are the real threats to God's people and God's kingdom of love.

We are living "in the meantime" between Jesus' first and second comings, and we are truly living "in the *mean* time" of the sinful human heart.

Miracles In The Meantime ...

Donald Woods' book, *Biko,* was published. Little by little the world heard and confronted the secret evils of apartheid, and we watched with astonishment as apartheid ended abruptly in 1990. President F. W. de Klerk proclaimed its formal end with the release of black leader Nelson Mandela after 28 years in prison and the legalization of black African political organizations. It was a miracle.

Apartheid crumbled, but evil still persists around us. Racial intolerance and ethnic cleansing continue throughout our world. Meanness is demonstrated in such things as school violence and road rage, domestic abuse and social disrespect.

As we face the evil of the world, we carry the end-times vigil into the twenty-first century. Although the kingdom of heaven is present in some ways with the coming of Jesus, its fulfillment remains primarily in the future. The cry heard through the centuries continues to go up, "How long?" How long must we wait?

In the meantime ... Doomsday prophets try to "seek out" God's secret codes and try to decipher when God will come out of "hiding" to establish the kingdom. But we are *not* playing a game of "end-times hide-and-seek" with God. Although it is intriguing to try to figure out when the end of the world will come, we cannot. "No one knows," says Jesus, "not even the angels or the Son, only the Father" (Matthew 23:36). This is not something we should worry about.

In the meantime ... we cannot hide in the basement, like little Andrew in a storm, only praying fearfully for our own salvation. Our concerns are bigger than ourselves.

In the meantime ... we may not sit passively and wait for divine intervention at the last to save us from ourselves and each other. Stephen Biko could not sit passively watching while apartheid killed his people. Donald and Wendy Woods could not sit passively hoping for apartheid's cruelty to end. They each had to *do something.* So do we.

In the meantime ... we must confront evil, even when dangerous. We must continue as long as there are places within our own lives and throughout the globe where love has grown cold. Our

44

courage and confidence are in God's powerful love, which overpowers and defeats evil. Miracles still occur.

In the meantime ... our job is to *claim* and *proclaim* this Good News! "... and then the end will come" (Matthew 24:14).

---

1. Richard Kyle, *The Last Days Are Here Again: A History Of The End Times* (Grand Rapids: Baker Books, 1998), p. 16.

Free? Indeed! The Continuing Reformation Of The Church

Julia, The Church Years

When she was one month old, Julia was baptized at Grace Lutheran Church. Her family came to church most Sundays. She progressed through every Sunday school classroom, and came faithfully even during fifth grade when they had to sit on chairs in the boiler room. She was confirmed in ninth grade and could recite most of the catechism, except sometimes she'd get mixed up on the meanings to the Lord's Prayer. She loved church.

On Sundays when she and her family slipped into their pew on the left-side middle of the church, Julia felt "at home" and secure. She'd make sure old Mrs. Griffin was in her spot somewhere behind them. She'd count all eight heads of the Sawyer kids, some barely visible above the pews ahead. If Mrs. Miller's Altar Guild's team was serving this month, every little wrinkle would be smoothed from the altar cloth and each candle would be exactly the same size. She felt a warm sense of belonging.

She felt a special bond with her friends who also went to church, any of the three churches in their rural Minnesota town. They could talk about things like babies getting baptized and how communion wafers stick to the roof of your mouth.

They liked to walk through the graveyards at each other's churches, and locate all the relatives they could identify. Her great-grandparents, her grandpa, and her uncle who died in the Vietnam War were buried right along the driveway as you drove into the parking lot at Grace. Even though they were dead, she liked to

47

imagine what it was like once upon a time when they sat in the pews inside.

Julia, The Dark Years

Then things changed. Julia moved far away after high school, and made some bad choices and terrible mistakes. She had several disastrous relationships, and had two children who were taken from her and placed into foster care. She even ended up in jail a couple times for shoplifting, because she didn't have the money for the fines.

After she got out of jail the second time, she was walking aimlessly one Sunday morning and stopped in front of a glassed-encased sign along a sidewalk. "Grace Lutheran Church," it said. "Everyone Welcome," it said. She remembered *her* Grace Lutheran Church, with its white steeple piercing the Minnesota sky so far away.

Without thinking, she went inside. The congregation was singing, "Amen" to the first hymn. The sweet smell of melting beeswax and fresh flowers brought back a comforting memory, and she sat down.

Then she looked around and felt ashamed. The worshipers around her looked like their lives were perfectly fine. She touched her hair nervously and pulled her jacket around her. She felt like "unfit mother" and "shoplifter" were written all over her. She didn't belong here.

Confession

She barely heard the pastor saying, "If we say we have no sin, we deceive ourselves ..." She heard the words repeated over and over, "We, we, we," but they didn't seem really to apply to the people she saw around her. She felt like the only sinner there. Even the people from *her* Grace Lutheran Church probably wouldn't want the likes of her in their pews anymore.

Of course, God could see what she couldn't see in the congregation around her: the swearing, swindling owner of the hardware store; the fifth grader who took money from his aunt's purse; the abusive mother; the teenage acolyte who despises her parents; the

48

man who is a brutal gossip at work as he claws his way up the ladder.

God saw into the heart of each worshiper, and Julia was certainly *not* the only sinner there. No one escapes sin.

Then everyone began to say together, "We confess that we are in bondage to sin and cannot free ourselves...." She was in bondage, all right — stuck in a life that felt all wrong. She was hardly the same person as little Julia who had never missed Sunday school back home. She wished there were some way back, or out. Julia joined in as the congregation said, "Forgive us, renew us, and lead us...."

When Julia lost her children and got caught shoplifting, her private sins had become very public. Both County Social Services and the Police Department had records on her and labels for her. She was starving for a chance to start over, but the future seemed hopeless, locked into this pattern of mistakes and failures.

She was very much like the woman who was hauled before Jesus and accused of adultery. This woman, too, was publicly accused of things done in private, was labeled for her sin, and things looked hopeless. Her accusers were ready to stone her to death.

But Jesus was able to free her! Jesus freed her from her accusers who couldn't claim arrogant perfection in front of him. Jesus freed her from the accusations that labeled her. Jesus freed her from her sin and its entrapping patterns. "Go, and sin no more," Jesus said to her (John 8:11 KJV).

Jesus could do the same for Julia.

Forgiveness

As Julia sat in church regretting her life, the pastor announced, "I declare to you the entire forgiveness of all your sins...." Would the pastor say those words so confidently if she knew who was sitting here? Julia wondered. She was so ashamed of her life that she was afraid to go home to Minnesota and hadn't been to church in years. It was probably a mistake to have come today, too.

Fifteen years ago on her Confirmation Sunday, Julia's class had recited Luther's meanings to the Apostles' Creed. Her part had been, "In this Christian church day after day he fully forgives my sins and the sins of all believers." She had practiced it and practiced it in front of the mirror and had raced through it flawlessly that day.

Back in ninth grade, the meaning to these words hardly seemed to matter much. Today with her life in shambles, the meaning to these words touched her imprisoned heart. Jesus forgives everyone in the church, including her!

She was in the company of sinners, but none of them had "outsinned" God's power to forgive. Forgiveness was announced to all of them. The Holy Spirit gently began to whisper good news into her tattered heart.

Free Indeed!

On this Reformation Sunday, we don't just celebrate an historical event. We celebrate God's *ongoing* reformation of lives through the freedom forgiveness brings.

Reading the New Testament, Martin Luther discovered that he didn't have to lie on a bed of nails to make up for his sins, and the church didn't have to sell indulgences to free souls from purgatory. Sitting in church that morning, Julia heard the assurance of God's forgiveness for her. She had a clean slate and a new chance. Jesus Christ, the Son, sets us free from our sins.

Jesus says, "Go, and sin no more." We are free. Free from the traps, lies, and disappointments of all our sins, public and private. Free from further accusation. Free to break the patterns and habits that keep the cycle of sin going. Free to go out and live life. Free. And if the Son makes us free, we will be free indeed.

There's an old story of a young man named Thomas, who was caught stealing sheep. The letters "ST" for "Sheep Thief" were branded into his forehead. Years went by, and though branded for his sin, he regained the respect of the villagers. He was the one who helped in any emergency, the one who would go out of his way to give someone a ride or a meal, the one who never judged anyone. He lived to be very old.

A young child saw him for the first time one day and asked his mother, "Mommy, what's 'ST' mean?"

The young mother answered, "I don't really know. Something happened many years ago, even before Grandma and Grandpa were born. But I think it stands for "Saint Thomas.""

Everyone has messed up and strayed from simple, child-like faith. God sets us free *from* our sins. And God sets us free *for* a new life.

Julia had stumbled into church that morning, but with God's forgiveness she now placed her foot on the road to freedom. She was freed to start in a new direction and had one thing to go on: "If the Son makes you free, you will be free indeed" (John 8:36).

She had a long way to go, but with God's forgiveness she would be freed from her sins again and again, day after day. *Her* Reformation was beginning ... and in that way, the Reformation of the church continues.

Thanks be to God!

All Saints' Sunday
Matthew 5:1-12

Jesus' Inaugural Address

Commotion At The Communion Rail

Tommy didn't budge.

When everyone else got up to leave the communion rail, he stayed kneeling. His folded hands were perched on the rail, and his little head was bowed so far down that his forehead was squinched against his thumb knuckles. His eyes were closed hopefully, as if he were waiting for a big present.

His mother gently touched his shoulder to nudge him along, but he just shook his head insistently. He wasn't going anywhere. Somehow the visiting pastor had forgotten about blessing the younger children when she went down the row giving communion, and he was still waiting.

The next group of people came up and knelt around him, and his embarrassed parents stepped off to the side. He waited with bowed head and closed eyes as the pastor came down the row again. Again, no blessing. Tommy stayed kneeling when the second group got up to leave.

People in their seats started wondering what was wrong. The communion servers were whispering to each other about what to do. Again his parents tried to get him to leave the rail, but he whispered loudly to them, "I didn't get blessed yet!" He wasn't going anywhere without his blessing.

The pastor heard him. She came over, placed both hands firmly on the little fellow's head, and blessed him. He looked up at her, beamed, and then skipped all the way back to his seat.

53

Tommy had come to the rail with hopes high and head bowed. He wanted to be blessed, and he wasn't going anywhere without it. That blessing lit up his face, lightened his step, and sent him happily on his way.

Commotion On The Mountainside

The same thing happened centuries ago on the side of a mountain.

Hopes were running high. Jesus was traveling through Galilee, curing people and preaching in their synagogues. He was gaining quite a following. His fame was spreading like wildfire.

People were coming from all over to hear him. When Jesus saw the crowds, he decided it was time for outdoor church. So he went up the mountain, sat down, and began preaching.

I can just imagine what happened as the crowd settled down on the mountainside to hear him. I can see people hurrying, pushing, and jockeying for the front-row seats nearest Jesus — aspiring leaders, prominent skeptics, and curiosity seekers. I can see the front rows closing in on Jesus, everyone hoping to make eye contact with him while he is speaking.

Behind these front-runners were "the rest of the people." Crowds of them.

Jesus' Inaugural Address

Jesus begins. "Blessed are the poor in spirit ... blessed are those who mourn ... blessed are the meek...." This is his great inaugural address for the kingdom that he is bringing. He carefully lays out what life is like under God's reign and summarizes the essence of his whole ministry. Line after line, he weaves together centuries of Jewish hope and prophecy, drawing them together in fulfillment.[1]

He meets the eyes of the front row with compassion and vision. They strategize for the front rows. They claw to the top. They step on the toes and dreams of others for their own advancement. In God's kingdom, it shall not be so. There is deliverance for them.

But Jesus doesn't stop there. His loving gaze and words of grace reach beyond the front rows, to the crowds behind.

"Blessed are the poor in spirit ..." A broken-spirited couple, who don't know if their children will eat tonight, look up.

"Blessed are those who mourn ..." The tear-streamed faces of widows and orphans look up.

Dozens of people in the cheap seats have come with hopes high and heads bowed. They have come wanting to be blessed, uncertain about life going anywhere from here. Person by person, Jesus lifts the heads and the hearts of those who can't — or don't dare — look up on their own. When Jesus speaks a blessing, they look up: the non-violent, gentle ones in the very back; those who hunger and thirst to see right prevail; those who give compassionately to the poor; those who have come out of heart-felt devotion to God; those who peacefully work for "shalom"; those ridiculed for taking a faith-filled stand on moral issues. There are no back-row seats in Jesus' kingdom. We are all drawn in, lifted up by grace, and blessed.

Inaugural address over, Jesus dismisses the crowds. The front rows vacate quickly. Some disperse into the crowds behind and others scurry away indignantly. Among the rest of the crowd, the air is filled with light-hearted chatter and excitement. People are walking with their heads held high and their steps lighter, maybe even skipping on their way back home. Hearts are bursting to tell cousins or neighbors that it's all true, everything they've heard about this Jesus.

And I imagine Jesus' gaze wandering from this hilly spot to another hill, looming on the horizon. Today it all begins on a hill and it will end on a hill, Golgotha. He knew he would die for them.

"Your Kingdom Come!"

Tommy had come to the communion rail with hopes high and head bowed. He wanted to be blessed, and he wasn't going anywhere without it. That blessing lit up his face, lightened his step, and sent him happily on his way.

The Beatitudes do the same for us.

Jesus has good news for those in the back: There are still no back-row seats in Jesus' kingdom. Listen, all of you who are branded "weak," or "naive," or "soft," or "foolish" by the world's standard bearers! The ridicule and disregard for you are mistaken. Lift up your heads! Jesus gives you a new label, "blessed." Wear it for all to see! The world's judgments have been overturned and replaced.

Jesus also has good news for those who always take the front-row seats: Your high-handed power plays and low-down maneuverings, your polish and prestige, are killing you. This fickle world holds you as its pawn. Look around and see that there are no back-row seats in the kingdom of God. Then you, too, will be truly "blessed." Jesus opens up a new path to you.

Jesus alone could topple the powers of this world and inaugurate such a kingdom as this. Not even the likes of James and John could assist, even though they offered (Mark 10:35ff). But he enlists us *all* for a spot in his cabinet. "Go, make disciples of all nations!" Spread this Good News to those who are downhearted and downtrodden, and to those who wield the world's power and authority.

Today is All Saints' Sunday in the church, and we remember those we love who have died and joined all the saints in glory. For them, this kingdom has come to fulfillment. But *we need not, we cannot, we will not* wait until heaven! The Beatitudes are just as much about earthly justice as they are about heavenly fulfillment.

On this side of glory, we keep vigil and continue to pray, "Your kingdom come."

- Until every child is fed, we will pray, "Your kingdom come!"
- Until every mourner is comforted, we will pray, "Your kingdom come!"
- Until the tyrants of this world no longer possess and exploit God's land and people, we will pray, "Your kingdom come!"
- Until God's justice prevails, we will pray, "Your kingdom come!"
- Until God's compassion guides us to acts of mercy, we will pray, "Your kingdom come!"
- Until we are single-mindedly devoted to God, we will pray, "Your kingdom come!"

- Until God's shalom helps us build bridges instead of walls, we will pray, "Your kingdom come!"
- And until the prophets of all time are vindicated, we will pray, "Your kingdom come!"
- Until each of these Beatitudes is fulfilled among us, we will pray, "Your kingdom come!"

Like Tommy, we come with hopes high and heads bowed. We want to be blessed and we're not going anywhere in life without it. The Beatitudes lift us to a new vision and send us on our way with a mission: the good news that this kingdom is drawing near.

"Your kingdom come, O Lord!"

---

1. Douglas R. A. Hare, *Matthew, Interpretation: A Bible Commentary For Teaching And Preaching* (Louisville: John Knox Press, 1993), pp. 33-35.

Thanksgiving
Luke 17:11-19

A Precious, Flickering Light

Lucille's Grief

A little baby girl was stillborn. Unfortunately, no one had anticipated problems going into delivery. Fifty years ago, when this happened, they didn't have the sophisticated technology to detect the particular problems this baby was having; her mother, Lucille, had gone under anesthesia expectant and hopeful.

She awoke a few hours later to the tragic news: there was no baby to hold, no cute little fingers and wiggling toes. Lucille never saw her precious little baby Martha, and they buried the baby during Lucille's ten-day hospital stay.

When Lucille finally came home from the hospital, all evidence of a baby had been removed from the house. Nothing was left of the preparations she had made so carefully for the baby — no nursery furniture, no baby clothes, no stroller, nothing.

Fifty years ago, pretending there had never been a baby seemed the best way to ease the pain. Lucille never saw her precious little Martha, and she came home from the hospital to life as usual.

But life was never usual after that. She never forgot that little daughter she loved so deeply but never saw and never held.

The years went by. Eventually she had another child, a son. She also loved him deeply but she never forgot her little baby girl.

Lucille and her husband and one son had a good life together. Forty years later Lucille's husband died and her beloved son lived far away. She had a lot of time to think. She thought a lot about little baby Martha, perhaps missing her more than ever before.

Lucille sometimes invited her good friend Bernice over for homemade soup, and they would have wonderful talks sitting at her kitchen table. Bernice didn't know about baby Martha. No one did.

One day Lucille was missing Martha very much, and vaguely mentioned her baby to Bernice. Little by little, over several lunches, she told more and more until one day she said, "You know, what really bothers me is that Martha never had a funeral."

Flickering In The October Wind

Bernice suggested they call their pastor and have a private funeral service out at little Martha's grave. Their pastor agreed and they set a time for the service one week later.

Lucille was both excited and nervous. She bought a special plant in memory of her daughter and set it in a sunny place in her living room. Pastor Kay and Bernice came over to her house and they planned the service carefully. Then on a bright October day, one week later, they headed out to the cemetery. Lucille brought flowers to leave at the grave, and Bernice brought a candle.

The Bible says the Spirit of God blows around us like the wind, and the Spirit was really blowing that day. They huddled together against the wind and thanked God for creating little Martha. They read special passages of thanksgiving and comfort from the Bible. They lit the candle to remember that, although Martha was unable to receive the gift of baptism in this life, she was still God's creation and loved by God.

Both Lucille and Bernice had to cup their hands around the candle to keep the wind from blowing out the flame.

They got to some of the most wrenching and hopeful words in the funeral service, the commendation. Loudly and into the wind Pastor Kay shouted, "Into your hands, O Merciful Savior, we commend little Martha." At that precise moment, with no change in the wind and hands still protecting the flame, it suddenly went out — as if someone had blown it out.

For a long time the three women looked at each other in silence. It was a holy moment. The Spirit of God was stirring with the wind, assuring Lucille, "Yes, little Martha is with me. Yes, she's fine. Yes, I love her and everything's all right."

Lucille's faith was as fragile as that candle flickering in the wind. That day she was like the ten lepers in the Bible who had also suffered much, perhaps also for many years. She and the lepers cried out to the mercy of almighty God for healing, as needed in their own ways: "Into your hands, O merciful Savior!" "Jesus, Master, have mercy!"

And God heard. God acted with mercy. God lifted their burdens and blessed them.

Lucille, Bernice, and Pastor Kay went back to Lucille's house after the service. They were all amazed at what had happened, and knew they had all sensed the same thing: the sure presence of God's comforting Spirit at that moment, at that little grave.

It was such a special experience that Lucille asked them not to tell anyone else about it. It would have been hard to explain what happened, and others might call it coincidence or dismiss it as if they were making much out of nothing. But they knew what they had experienced, as sure as the lepers who looked down and saw their skin healed.

Fifty years of silent grief began to lift from Lucille's shoulders that day. God had heard her; she felt sure of it. God loved her little Martha even more than she did. She no longer felt alone; God was in this with her. Lucille's heart felt lighter and her faith grew a little stronger. She was thankful.

Thank You, God!

You might wonder why I chose to tell a funeral story on Thanksgiving. It would be nice if our Thanksgivings were unclouded by the griefs and challenges of life, but that is seldom the case. That funeral service was really a service of giving thanks, and it was a mixture of all the complexity that makes up our Thanksgiving holidays as well.

Sometimes Thanksgiving celebrations feel inauthentic, when our burdens and losses almost mock us while we try to give thanks. Perhaps we are aware of the people missing from our Thanksgiving tables. Perhaps things tug at our hearts while we try to smile and celebrate. Perhaps we miss Thanksgivings past, or fear what the future holds. Perhaps we wonder how to give thanks when our cup feels *more* than half empty, or we feel empty inside. Sometimes we might *not* feel like giving thanks, and sometimes giving thanks might even seem inappropriate for our circumstances.

Fragile as a flickering candle in the wind, we may feel more like shouting into the air, "Jesus, Master, have mercy!" rather than, "Thank you!"

The healing of the ten lepers in the Bible and Lucille's story remind us that we are not just "blowing in the wind" when we cry out to God for mercy. When we commend ourselves and our concerns to the heavens, God hears. God acts mercifully. God gives us reason to give thanks, even in the middle of difficulties.

In the movie *Joe vs. the Volcano,* Joe is a life-long hypochondriac, stranded and dying on a raft floating in the ocean. Hungry, dehydrated, and half-delirious, he stirs in the night and sees the moon hovering over the water. It is huge and bright, practically covering the whole sky. He struggles to his feet. For the first time in his life, he has *perspective* on life.

Then he falls intentionally to his knees, crosses his arms over his chest, and does something he apparently hasn't done before: he prays. Quietly he says, "Dear God, whose name I do not know, thank you for my life! I forgot how big! Thank you. Thank you for my life."

The irony in this movie scene is powerful. Joe had spent most of his life so worried about dying that he never really *lived.* On the raft, actually facing death, he finally realizes what a gift it is just to be alive. Facing our losses and disappointments helps put our life and our priorities into perspective.

And when life falls into perspective, we fall to our knees — in thanksgiving.

Maybe this doesn't make sense to the world. Maybe nine out of the ten healed lepers just "thanked their lucky stars" that coincidence or fate put them in the right place at the right time.

Through the Bible, however, we *do* know who to thank. We see that it is *Jesus* who is active in the world, responsive to our needs, and powerful to help us. One leper met him on the road to healing; Lucille felt his Spirit blowing in the cemetery; we encounter him in many different ways. Along with Saint Paul, we may confidently claim, "I am convinced that neither death, nor life, nor angels, nor rulers, nor things present, nor things to come, nor powers, nor height, nor depth, nor anything else in all creation, will be able to separate us from the love of God in Christ Jesus our Lord" (Romans 8:38-39).

Commending ourselves again into the merciful arms of this faithful God, may we find the voice to say a simple, "Thank you. Thank you for my life. Thank you for my blessings."

Christ The King
Matthew 25:31-46

Facing Christ

Pilgrimage To A Bedside

First it was a seizure, then the tests, and then the deathblow diagnosis: inoperable brain tumor.

For the next year Jeanette, wife and mother of three young children, would show those around her how to live, as they watched her die.

When the tumor began its final rampage, she became bedridden. Her family set up a tiny bedroom for her next to the dining room of their old farm house. From there, she could hear the children practice piano on the old upright, or watch the family buzzing around the kitchen, or hear the children playing outside.

They were engaged in that farewell dance created by terminal illness: holding one another close, then flinging themselves apart, but never completely losing hold of each other's hands. Back and forth, in and out, life danced on while the clock ticked mercilessly forward. Jeanette cherished every minute.

Marion was one of Jeanette's many friends. It was hard for Marion to visit Jeanette, but not because of the illness. It was hard to visit Jeanette because, *in spite of her illness*, Jeanette was always doing the visiting. She'd ask about Marion's own three children, and how things were going at church and at work, and didn't Marion look a bit tired today? Like Jesus on the cross, taking care of his mother and even the thief hanging next to him, Jeanette cared for those around her.

Marion knew Jeanette appreciated their visits. But every time Marion left, she felt like *she* was the one who had been visited, not the other way around.

Jeanette became trapped in a body slowly shutting down, as the tumor trespassed into more and more of her brain. As if nailed down, her limbs became immobile. She nevertheless continued her spirit-filled way of living, graciously touching everyone around her with her faith and her gentleness. Slowly she commended into God's hands all that she was and all that she had.

So inspired by Jeanette's faith, Marion continued to feel like *she'd* been visited every time she came to see Jeanette.

Eventually silence replaced conversation. Jeanette would stir uncomfortably, and all Marion could do was to touch Jeanette's parched lips with a pink sponge dipped in water. Then Jeanette's eyes would thank her — deeply, sincerely, more profoundly than spoken words.

She continued to touch the depths of Marion's own soul.

Jeanette was teaching those around her how to live, as they watched her die: cherishing every moment; caring deeply about those around her; commending all of life to God; drinking thankfully of every drop of life.

Pilgrimages Of Reverse Mission

Jeanette's family chose Matthew 25:34ff to be read at her funeral. "Come, you that are blessed by my Father, inherit the kingdom prepared for you from the foundation of the world; for I was hungry and you gave me food, I was thirsty and you gave me something to drink, I was a stranger and you welcomed me, I was naked and you gave me clothing, I was sick and you took care of me ... Just as you did it to one of the least of these who are members of my family, you did it to me."

As Marion heard those words, she knew she had experienced them with Jeanette. A "reverse mission" had happened when she visited Jeanette; she had been visited as well. She and Jeanette had been to the cross together and had both been visited by Christ there. No wonder she had always left Jeanette feeling somehow touched by grace.

There's an organization called "Ministry of Money," which conducts trips they call "Pilgrimages of Reverse Mission." These are trips which help North American Christians understand the ministry they can do with their money — their disproportionately large percentage of global wealth. Ministry of Money sends people to places like Honduras, Haiti, and Gaza.

North Americans go on these trips from their privilege of wealth, expecting to *be* the body of Christ to people in need. But the reverse also happens: they *encounter* Christ through the people in need. These trips become, indeed, "pilgrimages of reverse mission."

For Marion, visiting Jeanette had been a vivid pilgrimage of reverse mission as she encountered Christ in Jeanette's suffering. For participants in "Pilgrimages of Reverse Mission" sponsored by Ministry of Money, people living in abundance encounter Christ among the poorest of the world. In both cases, the truth of Jesus' promise becomes enfleshed.

Marion began to see things — and people — differently after Jeanette's death. She began to *look* for Christ as she went about her daily activities, *looking* for opportunities to meet Christ by serving people around her. The distressed and needy are all around us. She took delight in allowing a hassled and hurried mother to go ahead of her in the grocery line. She found numerous occasions to send encouraging e-mails to co-workers. Rarely was there a day that didn't present some opportunity, now that her heart was looking for them.

Whether across the dinner table, across the street, or even across the globe, *life* is a pilgrimage of reverse mission. As Mother Teresa once said, "We can never do great things on this earth but we can do small things with great love."

"I got so much more than I gave." People often say that after a mission trip or after working on a Habitat for Humanity home. It's what one man said about his twenty years of volunteering at the nursing home and how one teenager felt about working in a special education classroom. When we reach out, we receive so much; we encounter Christ!

Facing Christ

Matthew 25 is devoted to three stories about the coming of the Son of Man for final judgment. This lesson, the third of these three, is about meeting Christ in suffering. It offers a surprising twist: while we wait for Christ's return, in a very real way Christ is already here — as the distressed and needy. Facing Christ does not just happen at the last judgment; it happens every day.

In surprising ways, both Jeanette and Marion became the face of Christ for each other. Jesus identifies with those who *go out* in mission. "Whoever welcomes you welcomes me, and whoever welcomes me welcomes the one who sent me" (Matthew 10:40). And in our Gospel lesson for today, Jesus identifies with the "least" in society. "... Just as you did it to one of the least of these who are members of my family, you did it to me" (Matthew 25:40). Christ works at both ends, bringing us together and blessing us in relationship to one another. We are part of a never-ending, ever-widening circle of grace.

But at the end of Matthew 25, Jesus is explicitly concerned about those who need help. Some of them may not be appealing or even receptive, and yet Jesus encourages us to acts of charity to the poor and lowly by linking himself to them. In God's abundant wisdom, facing Christ means really facing, really encountering each other.

This is good news for people hungering for God: seek God out through acts of mercy and justice, and you will meet Christ. If you want to find hope, build relationships with those who need help. Look around you, and you will begin to see Christ in the distressed and needy.

This is also good news for those suffering: God chooses you to wear the face and bear the grace of Christ to the world. When you are suffering, God has not abandoned you in your need. You are a special vessel of God's grace, even as God calls the world to your aid.

A couple years after Jeanette's death, Marion took a three-week work trip to an orphanage in Guatemala. She received a foreboding e-mail from the orphanage the night before she left: they were running out of food, they had few medical supplies left, and more children were arriving the same day as Marion and her co-workers. Still she didn't hesitate to go. "I know my heart is going to break, over and over again, when I get there," she said. "But I also know I will meet Christ in those little children, and that gives me hope."

Life is a pilgrimage of reverse mission, at home and across the globe. And always full of life-changing hope.

Lectionary Preaching After Pentecost

The following index will aid the user of this book in matching the correct Sunday with the appropriate text during Pentecost. All texts in this book are from the series for the Gospel Reading, Revised Common Lectionary. (Note that the ELCA division of Lutheranism is now following the Revised Common Lectionary.) The Lutheran designations indicate days comparable to Sundays on which Revised Common Lectionary Propers or Ordinary Time designations are used.

(Fixed dates do not pertain to Lutheran Lectionary)

Fixed Date Lectionaries *Revised Common (including ELCA)* *and Roman Catholic*	**Lutheran Lectionary** *Lutheran*
The Day of Pentecost	The Day of Pentecost
The Holy Trinity	The Holy Trinity
May 29-June 4 — Proper 4, Ordinary Time 9	Pentecost 2
June 5-11 — Proper 5, Ordinary Time 10	Pentecost 3
June 12-18 — Proper 6, Ordinary Time 11	Pentecost 4
June 19-25 — Proper 7, Ordinary Time 12	Pentecost 5
June 26-July 2 — Proper 8, Ordinary Time 13	Pentecost 6
July 3-9 — Proper 9, Ordinary Time 14	Pentecost 7
July 10-16 — Proper 10, Ordinary Time 15	Pentecost 8
July 17-23 — Proper 11, Ordinary Time 16	Pentecost 9
July 24-30 — Proper 12, Ordinary Time 17	Pentecost 10
July 31-Aug. 6 — Proper 13, Ordinary Time 18	Pentecost 11
Aug. 7-13 — Proper 14, Ordinary Time 19	Pentecost 12
Aug. 14-20 — Proper 15, Ordinary Time 20	Pentecost 13
Aug. 21-27 — Proper 16, Ordinary Time 21	Pentecost 14
Aug. 28-Sept. 3 — Proper 17, Ordinary Time 22	Pentecost 15
Sept. 4-10 — Proper 18, Ordinary Time 23	Pentecost 16
Sept. 11-17 — Proper 19, Ordinary Time 24	Pentecost 17
Sept. 18-24 — Proper 20, Ordinary Time 25	Pentecost 18

Sept. 25-Oct. 1 — Proper 21, Ordinary Time 26	Pentecost 19
Oct. 2-8 — Proper 22, Ordinary Time 27	Pentecost 20
Oct. 9-15 — Proper 23, Ordinary Time 28	Pentecost 21
Oct. 16-22 — Proper 24, Ordinary Time 29	Pentecost 22
Oct. 23-29 — Proper 25, Ordinary Time 30	Pentecost 23
Oct. 30-Nov. 5 — Proper 26, Ordinary Time 31	Pentecost 24
Nov. 6-12 — Proper 27, Ordinary Time 32	Pentecost 25
Nov. 13-19 — Proper 28, Ordinary Time 33	Pentecost 26
	Pentecost 27
Nov. 20-26 — Christ the King	Christ the King

Reformation Day (or last Sunday in October) is October 31 (Revised Common, Lutheran)

All Saints' Day (or first Sunday in November) is November 1 (Revised Common, Lutheran, Roman Catholic)

Books In This Cycle A Series

GOSPEL SET
It's News To Me! Messages Of Hope For Those Who Haven't Heard
Sermons For Advent/Christmas/Epiphany
Linda Schiphorst McCoy

Tears Of Sadness, Tears Of Gladness
Sermons For Lent/Easter
Albert G. Butzer, III

Pentecost Fire: Preaching Community In Seasons Of Change
Sermons For Sundays After Pentecost (First Third)
Schuyler Rhodes

Questions Of Faith
Sermons For Sundays After Pentecost (Middle Third)
Marilyn Saure Breckenridge

The Home Stretch: Matthew's Vision Of Servanthood In The End-Time
Sermons For Sundays After Pentecost (Last Third)
Mary Sue Dehmlow Dreier

FIRST LESSON SET
Long Time Coming!
Sermons For Advent/Christmas/Epiphany
Stephen M. Crotts

Restoring The Future
Sermons For Lent/Easter
Robert J. Elder

Formed By A Dream
Sermons For Sundays After Pentecost (First Third)
Kristin Borsgard Wee

Living On One Day's Rations
Sermons For Sundays After Pentecost (Middle Third)
Douglas B. Bailey

Let's Get Committed
Sermons For Sundays After Pentecost (Last Third)
Derl G. Keefer